Mint and the Blue Jay

By Sally Cowan

"What is on the menu, Dad?" said Mint.

"Oh, we ran out of nuts on Tuesday," said Dad.

"That's true," said Mint.

Mint got a big case
to get more nuts.

In no time at all,
Mint had **loads** of nuts.

She chewed a few of them!

“Hi!” called Mint’s new pal, Peggy Sue the newt.

“Hi, Peggy Sue!” Mint called back.

While Mint was not checking, a sneaky blue jay flew down and stole a nut!

“I have so much news!”
said Peggy Sue.

Mint and Peggy Sue had a long chat.

The blue jay flew down to take more and more nuts!

“I must get these nuts home for the stew,” said Mint.

I did not chew them all!

“This bright blue quill is a clue!” said Peggy Sue.

Mint had to get more nuts for the stew.

She was mad at that blue jay!

CHECKING FOR MEANING

1. What were Mint and Dad planning to do with the nuts Mint collected? *(Literal)*
2. Why did Mint have to collect the nuts twice? *(Literal)*
3. How would you describe the blue jay? *(Inferential)*

EXTENDING VOCABULARY

stew	What is a stew? Have you ever eaten a stew? What is the difference between a stew and a soup?
newt	Look at the word *newt*. What sounds are in this word? What is a newt? Where might you find one?
clue	What does the word *clue* mean? How did the clue in the story help Mint? When might you need a clue?

MOVING BEYOND THE TEXT

1. Do you think it was Mint's fault that the blue jay took her nuts? Why?
2. What are some other foods that blue jays might eat?
3. What ingredients would you use if you were making a stew?
4. When have you helped at home? What did you do?

TIME TO WRITE

Write about how Mint felt about having most of her nuts taken by the blue jay.

PRACTICE WORDS

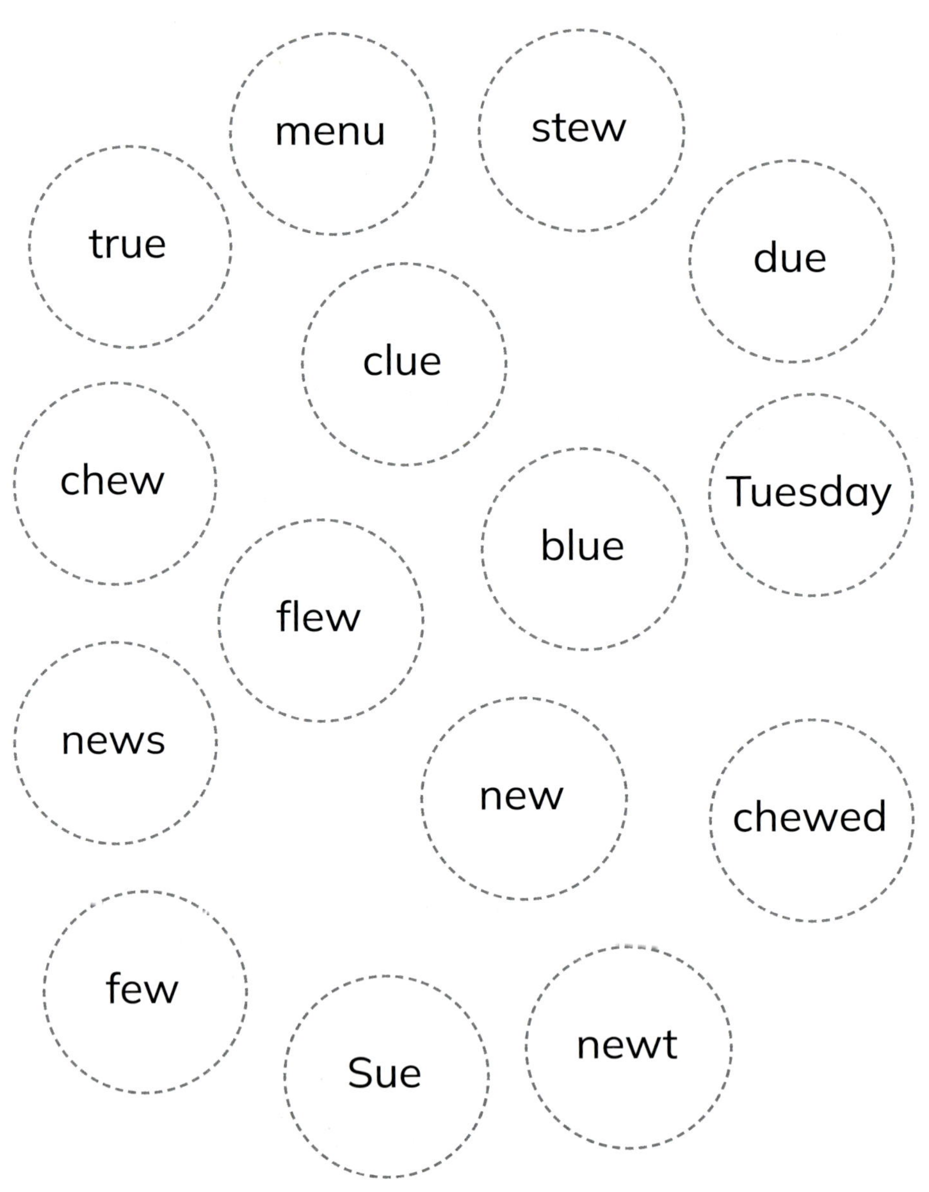